Saturday Mornings

Written by Joelie Hancock

Illustrated by Fred Willingham

First published in the United States of America in by
MONDO Publishing
By arrangement with MULTIMEDIA INTERNATIONAL (UK) LTD

Printed in China
Everbest Printing (Guangzhou, China), Co. Ltd-12033

ISBN 978-1-57255-059-9

Originally published in Australia by Horwitz Publications Pty Ltd
Original development by Robert Andersen & Associates and Snowball Educational

Designed by Christy Hale

I love Saturday mornings.

My brother washes the car,

and I often help.

My grandpa works in the garden,

and I often help.

My sister washes the clothes,

and I often help.

My dad mops the floors,

and I often help.

Sometimes my mom cleans out the garage,

and I often help.

But when my grandma cooks in the kitchen,

I ALWAYS help.